Know How to Make Your Own Latex & Silicone Soap & Candle Moulds

By

Kerri Newbury

Moorna Publications

ISBN: 978-0- 9872715-3-2

Book titles in Kerri Newbury's 'Know how to Make' series are:

Know How to Make Candles

Know How to Make Cold Process Soap

Know How to Make Liquid Soap

Know How to Make Your Own Latex & Silicone Soap & Candle Moulds

All of these crafter's books are available through the same bookstore outlet where you purchased this book.

All Kerri Newbury's 'Know How to Make' book series are proudly published by **Moorna Publications**.

Special thanks to Andrew & Peter

Book Contents:

Introduction

Because my daughters and I own and operate an ever expanding CP soap and candle making business we have become avid mould collectors and users.

These tend to be mainly made from latex and silicone these days, and we use them on an almost daily basis in both our 'standard' and 'novelty' poured candle, and CP soap making production.

Our mould collection began much as any other soap and candle maker's would do, by purchasing the rigid vacuum formed plastic types from various sources around the world, but we soon found that rigid plastic moulds have huge limitations, while not standing up to the high working temperatures often required.

Luckily for us, a steadily increasing source of ready to use latex and silicone moulds began trickling onto the marketplace. These opened up a whole new dimension to our craft, but this too had limitations, the main part of that being the very often high prices of such moulds.

While the sum of anywhere between $4.00 and $12.00 per mould may not seem a big deal when you are only buying the odd single mould now and then for personal use, it begins stacking up as a huge investment in production costs when you need to be able to produce fifty or more of the same moulded candle or soap in just the one pour, just to keep up with your customer order demands, and that's only just for one particular design at a time.

Then once you begin multiplying that one design at a
cost of an average of $600.00 worth of moulds at a time by a couple or more hundred designs you find yourself wondering how you will ever recoup the thousands of dollars in mould outlay when you must stay competitive in your chosen marketplace.

At one stage we worked it out that with all the various 'bought in' moulds we had somewhere around $28,000.00 tied up in our ever expanding business, without taking into consideration all the other tooling costs for everything else we are involved in.

No matter whom you are, that's a lot of money sitting around tied up!

The question we needed to find an answer to was, 'How can we cut down on mould purchasing costs without cutting back on quality, necessary replacements, and new product lines?"

Rather foolishly, neither my daughters nor I recognised that the answer was right under our noses all the time.

It came in the shape of my husband Andrew, who had suffered a bit of a health scare, and had been a working lifetime engineering Tool Fitter, and my youngest daughter's husband Peter, who at the time, was a Fibreglass Laminator working for a boat manufacturing company.

Both of them had held the desire to work for themselves for longer than any of us girls could remember, but both of them shied away from the huge costs involved in starting up their own businesses.

Their joint venture began in a very small way as a hobbyist kind of thing, through creating our much needed replacement latex moulds using readily available for purchase liquid 'brush on' latex rubber, but soon they had expanded into turning out our replacement silicone moulds too, and all at a fraction of the costs of buying them in from our previous mould supply sources.

The added bonus to us with Peter was that he had been a lifetime model maker of miniature resin figurines of all descriptions. These he had always created from scratch by meticulously carving them out of wood and plaster first.

So before we knew it Peter was creating brand new custom designed 3D soap and candle making moulds for us to try out.

Once they had been tried and tested in the odd one's and two's, Andrew and Peter quickly turned those moulds out in quantities that astounded us, and our soap and candle production lines went into overdrive.

To cut a long story short …

Andrew and Peter now jointly own and operate a large, and rapidly expanding, latex and silicone mould making business, supplying thousands upon thousands of soap, candle, plaster, concrete and resin moulds to resellers around the world.

I would have no doubt that those soap and candle makers who have used ready made latex and silicone moulds from various global retailers, will have used at least one of Andrew and Peter's products without ever being aware of where in the world they were made and supplied to the retailer from.

That's how big a business they have created

from starting out working in their backyard sheds.

The happy ending for my daughters and I is that we now pay far less for our soap and candle moulds - we buy them direct from my husband and son-in-laws business - while having a far larger range of them than ever before, some exclusive to our own soap and candle manufacturing business.

That happy ending doesn't finish quite there, because with the very able assistance of my husband and son-in-law I am now able to write this book so as to be able to teach any willing reader of it, How to Make Your Own Latex & Silicone Soap & Candle Moulds.

The even happier thing is that it's not as hard as one may think it to be!

Here's to your success,
Kerri

Creating latex moulds from everyday objects.

This is the same point that my husband and son-in-law started out from, and it's the easiest starting point for anyone else to begin, the creation of your own latex moulds using store bought candles, bars of soap, or even just about any object you fancy reproducing for your own future craft efforts.

The only reason I hold back the word EVERY object you fancy turning into a mould isn't because anything is impossible, as it is perfectly possible, but if you wish to be able to light up and burn your candles they need to be created in a 'block' shape, but if you aren't worried about being able to use them for the reason they are created as candles for, you are only limited by your imagination.

The other proviso with both candles and soaps is that if you create moulds that have very tiny weak points, such as tiny individual fingers or animal whiskers etc. you will never get them back out of your moulds in one piece. Needing to constantly clean tiny bits of wax or soap out of your moulds is a real pain, so it's better to just avoid the need to do so right from the very start.

Other than that you can turn out very finely detailed soaps and candles of all kinds.

So let's begin ….

First of all you need to gather together your required toolkit, and these and the items you should have in it:

A paintbrush or two
A craft knife or similar
Some light dishwashing liquid.
Disposable cups – clean plastic yogurt containers are ideal for the job.
A rolling pin or something that can be used as one.
Some plasticine or play dough, or similar
6mm narrow strips of wood – you'll understand what these are for as you read on.
A sheet or two of stiff plastic sheeting or waxed paper.

That deals with your toolkit, but then you'll also need something that you wish to use to create your casting mould out of, and for this example I will talk about a simple 50mm diameter by 100mm length piece of wooden dowel that has been sanded finely and sealed with timber sealant so that it is non-porous.

Now we'll discuss the preparation before the application of any liquid latex:

By now, no doubt you'll be asking yourself, "What do I need bits of wood and play dough or plasticine for?"

Here comes the answer …

The strips of wood are to place on your workbench as thickness guides and levelling tools, so everything stays nice and even when you roll out the plasticine or play dough, which we will later stand our dummy or 'Master' candle upright upon, ready to be latex painted.

But first things first ....

The plasticine or play dough - both are cheaply purchased or homemade non-hardening modelling clay forms and we'll use plasticine for this example – will create a vital part of your finished new mould, in fact you'll be struggling to use the mould at all if it isn't there to begin with, as it'll become the way you can suspend the mould upside down while you're pouring the candle wax, or liquid soap, into the space you have created from the length of wooden dowel – the master item - as your candle or soap bar.

Let's make our first mould ...

First, place a piece of waxed paper or stiff plastic sheet on your work surface, then lay your strips of wood down on top of it, around 100mm parallel apart for this example.

Next, soften your guessed at measured out portion of plasticine between the pieces of wood and roll the plasticine out to that same thickness and evenness, then put the wood strips aside.

Trim the overall size of the flattened plasticine down so it measure approx 100mm square surface area – or gently place a cup or similar on top of the plasticine and trim around it to create a round level base.

That base will now be an even 6mm thick, plenty thick enough for its eventual purpose as an upturned suspension platform.

This lip will also make your mould far easier to

handle when it comes to de-moulding times of your candles or soaps.

Now place your master item centrally on top of the base and press it into the surface very lightly.

This action just creates a leak proof seal between the master item and the mould base.

Now we're ready to begin latex painting.

NB. Liquid latex MUST always be used in a well ventilated work area.

These latexes are air drying, but they allow you plenty of time to work with them, so don't panic.

It is essential that your first layer is applied thinly, as this allows you to easily see any air bubbles trapped in the latex as you apply it.

The better the job you make of this very first coat, the better quality your final mould will be, and in turn the better quality, and/or more finely detailed of eventual candle or soap bar you'll turn out from that mould.

Now shake the bottle of latex well so as to ensure no separation of liquids and solids has occurred, then, pour just a little liquid latex into a disposable cup pick up your paintbrush, and away we go.

Before you begin applying the latex, first put some of your light dishwashing liquid onto the bristles of your paint brush. Squeeze out the excess because all this is for is to help keep the bristles from clogging up, then later making it easier to wash your brush out in water when you are finished applying the latex.

You don't actually paint the latex onto anything as it's quite thick, you only move it around over your plasticine mould base and master item as evenly as possible, without air bubbles being trapped in it as you work.

Again I stress the need for a thin coat of latex as your first coat, and the need to keep it as free of air bubbles as possible.

With our example master item the complete job would take a newbie at the task maybe 5 to 10 minutes at tops, but once you become far more confident you'll find such a small, simple mould form takes around 2-3 minutes at this stage.

Note: Wash your paintbrush out immediately, never leave it until later or you will be forever buying new paintbrushes as replacements.

You will not touch your work again for at least two hours.

Once you have the first coat dry you can begin really going for it, as you have more coats to apply with breaks for drying time in between each coat.

Note: Every brand of liquid latex is different, so be sure to read the instructions regarding drying times etc. before starting work.

My husband recommends a minimum of two hours in between latex coats, but also adds that the longer the better, up to four hours.

In its liquid form latex is white, and as it dries it becomes more of a milky coffee/caramel brown colour.

It is important to ensure that no white spots remain in the latex before your next coat is applied.

You will need a minimum of 10-15 layers of latex in total – some people suggest as many as 20 layers.

When the final layer of latex has been applied and has thoroughly dried out it's time to de-mould it from your master item.

To do this …

Firstly, carefully remove the waxed paper if you have used it, taking care not to shred it as it will just make it harder to get it all off the mould.

If you used a piece of stiff plastic sheet such as one of those clear plastic document covers you can purchase from any stationary supplier you only need to carefully remove it now.

Next, apply a little dishwashing liquid over the outside of your new mould. – This is to prevent the mould sticking to itself as you remove it from your master item, just as you might roll off a rubber glove from your own hand.

It is for this reason that latex moulds are commonly referred to as being 'Glove moulds'.

Your latex mould is now ready for use.

Notes: Don't think your moulds will last forever because they won't. On average we have found that each mould will produce about fifteen products before they begin to break up, then you need to make a replacement for it. It's why we were so horrified at the ongoing cost of mould purchases at one time.

Never add stearine to paraffin wax for use in latex moulds. Stearine is an acid and eats latex moulds like you would never believe possible.

To help extend the life of your mould always store it in a dark place, and always apply some dishwashing liquid to the outside before de-moulding your items.

Creating silicone moulds from everyday objects

I shall be splitting this section of the book into three distinct and separate sub-sections further on.

This is because it's both easier to deal with each sub-section separately, and also far less confusing to the reader, but before doing so I will talk about the creation of silicone moulds in general terms to save repeating myself later, and thereby unnecessarily increasing the length of this book.

The sub-sections will teach you how to create three totally separate silicone mould types, the first being 'Flat backed' moulds, the second being 'Two part' moulds, and the final section being 'Custom' moulds.

Unlike latex mould making, which uses a 'single piece liquid product' that requires multiple applications with drying time between each and every layer/coat, silicone mould making uses a 'two part liquid product' that is applied in the one single pour.

Whereas the latex mould creation takes very little time in the preparation stage, but heaps of time in the actual creation stage, silicone is the absolute opposite, meaning that the most time is used up during the preparation stage while the creation stage takes very little time by comparison.

However, the time spent in preparation with silicone mould making will pay dividends in the end because it will both save you money, and you'll end up with a finely detailed, better quality mould for your efforts.

The money saving part of the deal comes into play
when you carefully plan the eventual thickness of the mould walls itself, as liquid silicone is NOT a cheap product to purchase in the first place, unlike liquid latex by comparison.

The thickness of the mould will also have a huge effect on its flexibility, with a mould created with a too thicker wall being far more rigid, and in turn, far more difficult to use at product de-moulding times, especially with items that are deeply undercut.

The advantage of silicone moulds over latex moulds is their working life expectancy.

A silicone mould's lifespan well exceeds that of a latex mould.

Once again, every liquid silicone manufacturer will vary their product composition, so no two are exactly the same to work with, so ensure that you read each manufacturer's measuring and mixing procedure carefully before use.

Also once again, ensure you always work with liquid silicones in a well ventilated area.

Another must is ensuring that you wear suitable eye safety wear in case of splashes etc.

The beauty of using liquid silicone is that you can use a master item made out of virtually any type of material, Leather, Metal, Concrete, Wax, Non-hardening oil based clay, Hard water clay, Plaster etc.

Now let's discuss you toolkit …

These are the sorts of items you need in it before starting work into silicone mould making:

When working in larger quantities of liquid silicone you will need a decent electronic scale - battery powered or mains powered – that shows weights in grams and kilos.

Eye safety goggles

Latex gloves

Craft knife

Tape measure or rule

Pencil or small diameter maker pen

Palette knife

Sealer

Disposable stirring sticks

Conical measuring cup for the catalyst

Bluetac or similar temporary fixing putty

Disposable mixing plastic containers

Hot melt gun

Ceramic clean-up tool

Conical measuring cups for use with small amounts of liquid silicone base – use the scale when working with larger amounts.

G-clamps or quick release clamps.

Mould box making material – you can use melamine coated particle board, Corflute, cut down cleaned and dry plastic soft drink bottles, even your kid's Lego building blocks, just don't tell them about it.

The correct type of silicone release agent for the manufacturer's product you will be using.

That'll just about cover the toolkit side of things.

Note: Some of the above items are optional as you see later on.

Now let's get into talking about moulding box preparation:

All that is required to make yourself a moulding box is a base sheet of melamine coated particle board so that your finished mould can be removed from it fairly easily.

Other than that you only require four sides that can be held together firmly by either clamps - or in the case of Lego bricks just clipped together.

You need to make the base surface area of the mould box the minium of the size of your master casting item, plus at
least 5cm extra all around.

The height of your silicone pouring area of the mould box should measure the height of the master casting item, plus 3cm minimum in total.

Flat backed silicone moulds

This is by far the best way to begin for a newbie to silicone mould making.

Flat backed moulds are perfect for creating soaps or candles etc. that sit on their own base. Items such as upright open flowers and conical bee hives are prime examples.

Mould casting preparation is carried out in the following way:

Fasten your master item to the moulding box base – this should always be 12-18mm thick melamine coated particleboard - using either your Bluetac applied in a thin rolled ribbon around the base of your master item, or if you have one, a hot glue gun, by running a bead of glue around the base of the master item a few millimetres from the edge. Liquid latex can also be used by just dabbing a little onto the centre of the master item's base.

Just fix the master item onto the centre of the base of the moulding box by applying light pressure.

This flattens your choice of temporary adhesive out while at the same time forming a tight seal beneath your master item so as to prevent leakages of silicone getting in beneath it.

Remove any adhesive that has squeezed out between your master item and the mould box base.

Before continuing onto the next step you should inspect the seal between the moulding box base and the master item to ensure there are no gaps. If there are any, simply fill them in with a tiny bead of Bluetac and press it into the gap to seal it off completely – a ceramic clean-up tool is perfect for this job.

If the master item is made from a very porous material it should be vented beneath it in order to prevent air that may become trapped in, or on the master item, from forcing its way into the silicone by way of bubbles.

To do this simply drill a couple of small holes through the mould box baseboard before affixing your master item to it as it's far easier to do this at such a stage while you can still view everything clearly.

If your master item is made out of particularly porous materials, such as plaster, wood or leather etc. you should apply several coats of sealer to it with drying time in between, and then allow it to dry out thoroughly before using it for this task.

You are now ready to construct your moulding box walls.

Begin by applying a bead of glue or latex along the bottom edge of one of the side walls and fix it to the moulding box base board, remembering to keep a gap of 1cm, from the closet point of your master item. This is called the mould wall thickness.

This is what you need your pencil or marker pen and rule for, to mark things out before you begin constructing your side walls of the moulding box.

The other side walls can now be fixed into place in exactly the same way as the first was, but additionally, a bead of adhesive should be applied to the end edges of the remaining side walls so they also become glued to each other.

All joints around the inner sides of the moulding box need to be sealed with non-hardening putty such as Bluetac to prevent leakages of liquid silicone during casting.

Always double check to ensure all joints in your moulding box are totally sealed off from leaking.

Finally measure a distance of 1cm above the highest point of your master item and mark the same height up from the moulding box base and mark it on the side wall where you can clearly see it during pouring time.

Note: If you are making a mould from a very small master item the quickest and simplest thing to use for your moulding box walls is a cut down plastic drink bottle sealed to the base board.

This can be fitted to a rolled out piece of play dough or plasticine in the same manner as you prepared the base of a latex mould.

This time however you simply press the lower cut edge of the cut down plastic bottle about half way into the plasticine or play dough to create the leak proof base seal around your master item.

Applying mould release to your moulding item and box:

Most moulds will not need mould release with silicone, but it is a good idea to use it until you have developed a greater experience in the job.

The entire surface of the moulding box and the master item should now have a thin coat of soft paraffin, Vaseline or recommended mould release agent applied.

When using a liquid mould release agent you should always allow the carrier fluid in it to fully evaporate before proceeding.

The correct mould release agent should be used according to the silicone manufacturer's specifications.

Never be tempted to use spray vegetable oils, mineral oil or spray lubricants such as WD40 etc.

Ready to pour:

Measure out and mix your two part liquid silicone according to the manufacturer's instructions.

You will require sufficient silicone to completely fill in the full space between the moulding box wall and the master item, and right up to the mark you placed on the wall before preparing for your pour.

Most often this part of the task is guessed at, even by professional mould makers.

Always make sure that you mix the two parts of the silicone liquid together thoroughly. This becomes fairly obvious with most manufacturers' silicone products, as they will change to an even colour at that point, instead of the base part being usually white, and the catalyst being a coloured liquid.

It is advisable to measure your base liquid out into a container that you reserve for the purpose, and mix it in a disposable one.

Pouring time:

When pouring mixed silicone into a moulding box it should always be poured into the lowest part of the box in a thin steady stream, and permitted to rise up around the master item so that the liquid displaces the air as it rises up the box. This helps to eliminate air entrapment.

Pour from a reasonable height above the moulding box so that it allows air bubbles within the mixing container to pop.

Note: Always make sure that the moulding box is on a level plane before pouring begins - using a small spirit level if necessary.

Continue pouring until the upper level of the liquid silicone reaches the mark you made on the inside of your moulding box wall.

It is nigh on impossible to guess this level if you failed to mark it out before pouring begins, but the thickness is vitally important to the finished mould.

I have given the reasons for this earlier in this book.

Any air bubbles rising to the surface of the poured silicone can be dissipated by lightly passing a heat blowgun or hair drier quickly over the surface.

Leave the poured moulding box at room temperature overnight to cure, which is when the liquid has become a flexible solid.

De-moulding:

After the silicone has cured, your master item can be removed from your newly created mould.

To do this first remove the moulding box side walls by breaking the glue seams holding it tight.

Next break the seal between the master item and the moulding box base board.

This is most easily done by using your palette knife.

Slide it in between the mould box base and the base of your master item and new mould and twist it slightly so the action causes the two things to separate from each other cleanly.

Your master item can now be popped out of the new silicone mould.

This is best achieved by gently pushing the flexible silicone away from the master item while working your fingers and thumb around the master item gradually while getting deeper and deeper until the master item eventually completely releases itself from the mould.

You are now the proud owner of your first self made flat backed silicone mould.

Well done!

Two part silicone moulds

Now that we have covered the flat backed mould making procedure this 'upmarket' version of the same sort of thing will be a walk in the park.

I won't bother going through the moulding box construction process again as you will already know what you're doing there now.

So let's get straight into things shall we?

This type of silicone mould is called a 'Two piece block mould' because you are totally enclosing your master item in silicone. However, the mould is created as two separate components.

The reason why these types of moulds are created is normally due to the fact that the master item has detail all the way over it, eg. A golf ball with those little dimples all over it.

To begin:

For this example we are going to use a golf ball as our master item, as we have found that this shape of soap is a big seller in packs of three with a couple of golf tees as gifts for golfers, both male and female.

So our first task is to select a moulding box that is big enough to contain the complete golf ball across its spherical diameter, plus 3cm minimum so as to allow for the mould wall thickness at the narrowest point on every side.

We start off by fixing the golf ball onto a flat surface with a tiny dab of hot melt glue so it will remain perfectly still while we measure around it and place marker points at it's halfway height point with a fine marker pen.

This gives us the exact position of where the two halves of the final mould will split apart when de-moulding time comes around whilst soap making.

Now we need our non-hardening clay such as play dough.

We fill our moulding box up to just below the half way point using our clay/play dough, making as neat a job of it as possible so our first half of our future silicone mould has a nice smooth, level surface ready to meet to the second half of the mould during soap casting.

Next, gently, but firmly push the golf ball into the clay until it is embedded in the clay to the level of the marks you so carefully put around the ball earlier.

Ensure that the clay is a snug, leak free fit around both the inner moulding box walls, and the golf ball so silicone will not run into any gaps between them.

Now we need to create 'registration keys':

These are the little knobs around the edge of the future mould that will ensure that the two halves of your final mould will fit together perfectly every time you use it to cast soap golf balls from.

You can create these keys in either of two ways, the first being by simply indenting a little distance in from each corner of the clay around the ball with the blunt end of a pencil so it creates a 'female' half of the key in the clay.

The other way, and the way our professional mould making team create them is by pushing small steel balls into each corner of the clay so they create a 'male' key half protruding out of the clay.

1cm dia polished ball bearing balls are the perfect tool for the job in a mould this size, and they are fully re-usable
afterward.

The next thing to do is to cut a length of plastic tube around the diameter thickness of a pencil that fits snugly between one of the closest point of the golf ball to the moulding box inner wall, and press it into the clay so it becomes halfway submerged.

Always ensure that the tube is in contact with your master item.

This will eventually become the filler feeder point to your 2 part mould.

Now apply your preferred mould release agent, i.e. Vaseline or manufacturer's recommended mould release agent.

Note: Make sure you allow the fluid to evaporate off before continuing on.

Now measure out and mix your two part silicone liquid according to the manufacturer's instructions and pour it into the moulding box in the same manner as you did with your flat backed mould casting.

Set the job aside to allow the silicone to cure fully before moving onto the second half of your two part mould.

Now we move onto completing the job:

Remove the master item **and** poured half of your mould from the moulding box, turn the mould over and remove your clay/play dough.

Reposition the moulded half of your new golf ball mould back into the moulding box and ensure it seals well around the edges between the inner box walls and the already made first half of your mould.

Remove the ball bearing registration keys if you have used them, but ensure your filler feeder tube remains snugly in place against the golf ball master item which is still embedded in the poured half of your mould.

Coat all moulding surfaces with mould release as before.

Measure and mix your two part silicone liquid as before, and pour the second half of your new two part mould.

Leave the newly poured silicone to cure.

Time for de-moulding:

Remove the complete mould from the moulding box and separate the two halves. Carefully trim away any 'flashing' from the mould.

Remove your master item in the same way as you did with the flat backed mould master item.

You now own your first personally made two part silicone casting mould.

Now do your mould maker's victory jig!

Notes: Casting into a two part mould:

To cast into your new two part mould ensure that both halves of the mould are fully located and locked together via the registration keys.

Secure mould together with a rubber band or masking tape.

Pour in a small quantity of the casting medium - soap/wax – place a finger over the filler channel and carefully rotate the mould in all directions to ensure that all the fine details within the mould walls become coated fully with your casting medium.

Continue pouring your casting medium into the mould, but ensue you tilt the mould now and then to allow the air to escape out of it as you go.

You can cut additional air escape channels into your mould if needs be.

These can be plugged off as you work in the casting stage to prevent further escape of your casting medium once you see the medium coming out of the gaps.

After your cast has set fully you open the mould, remove the new product and trim away the cast pouring channel spout, any flashings and additional air escape spouts, and your product can be set aside for curing etc.

Custom silicone moulds

The final section of this book deals with the creation of custom making moulds to suit personal requirements in bars of soap etc. Designs such as trade names and so forth.

This means creating a mould that will turn out bars of soap or candles with a particular design or name indented into their outer surface/s.

These goods may be produced using either a flat backed, or two part mould, dependant upon the shape of the bar of soap or candle you wish to create.

The mould making principles are exactly the same as those earlier discussed in this book; it's only the way in which you create the required customised 'Signature' that this section deals with.

For this example we will use the word ....

CASTILE

The first thing you will require is a ready cast plaster 'form blank' of your soap bar shape to work with.

Prepare your design as a mirror image - back to front – transfer on your computer, and print it out on your inkjet printer, or any type of printer that uses water based ink - you'll know it's water based if the ink bleeds when it gets wet – in BLUE when you are satisfied that it looks exactly as you wish it to do.

Blue ink transfers far better than black ink does for this task.

Place your transfer face down on top of your dampened plaster soap bar blank - with the face you're working on dry - so that it reads correctly when looking down on it from the top.

Press on the transfer gently with a moistened finger, but not wet, only moist.

You only need to dampen the transfer enough as you work until the design shows through the back of the paper and is not bleeding horizontally.

If the design bleeds horizontally you are making the paper too wet, or your plaster blank is too wet.

You should use enough pressure on the transfer so that it sticks to the plaster blank temporarily.

Once you are sure that the ink has bled lightly into the plaster blank you can remove your transfer, but then you need to work fast, but carefully, before the ink begins to fade away. As it will as the surface of the plaster dries out.

It's best to engrave around the very edge of the design first so that if the ink fades away while you're working on the inner part of the engraving you will still have the outline of it clearly showing to continue working within.

This will allow you all the time you need to complete your engraving if the engraving is complicated.

When making a deep engraving it's better to work at it a little bit at a time as it avoids the risks of breaking away bits of the plaster you work that wish to remain in the bar surface.

It is why you work with a dampened plaster blank rather than a totally dry one.

Your choice of engraving tool is up to you.

When you have completed the engraving rinse the debris from off the plaster blank and sit it face uppermost on a dry towel to dry out thoroughly.

Never towel dry the blank as this will cause pieces of lint to stick to it which will become embedded in your future mould design, and they look unprofessional and ugly as they show up as bumps and dents.

By just sitting the blank on a towel it causes the moisture in it to be drawn downward, drying the upper levels out first.

Once your plaster blank is 100% dry you are ready to seal it and create your chosen type of silicone mould from it, using either method described earlier in this book.

Notes: When making soap in silicone moulds always ensure that engravings and design indentations are pre-lubricated to help prevent air bubbles becoming trapped at these points.

Silicone moulds are not great insulators, so most soap makers will adjust things in cooler climes to ensure full gelling takes place during the soap making process.

These final pages are dedicated to the use of jotting down your own personal notes on your mould making experiences. It pays to keep a record of weights and measures you use when creating your moulds so that you do not waste expensive materials. Better you pay for a few pages of extra paper now than pay out hundreds of dollars in materials you throw in the trashcan later.

Personal notes and observations

Personal notes and observations

Personal notes and observations

Personal notes and observations

Personal notes and observations

Printed in Great Britain
by Amazon.co.uk, Ltd.,
Marston Gate.